A STUDY GUIDE TO
TAKE YOU DEEPER INTO

Victorious
SPIRITUAL
WARFARE

So Simple, Grandma Can Do It!

MAUREEN BRODERSON

Copyright 2024 by MAUREEN BRODERSON

Published by Leadership Books,
Inc. Las Vegas, Nevada – New York,
New York
LeadershipBooks.com

ISBN:
978-1-951648-42-8 (Paperback)
978-1-951648-98-5 (eBook)

All Rights Reserved. No part of this publication may be reproduced, distributed, or transmitted in any form or by any means, including photocopying, recording, or other electronic or mechanical methods, without the prior written permission of the publisher, except in the case of brief quotations embodied in critical reviews and certain other noncommercial uses permit-ted by copyright law.

WHAT'S BEING SAID ABOUT THIS STUDY GUIDE...

In this thoughtful and well-designed companion guide, the life-giving principles laid out in "Victorious Spiritual Warfare, So Simple, Grandma Can Do It" are offered as a transformative resource to anyone seeking to grow stronger and deeper in their Christian faith. Maureen Broderson's work here is a wise, insightfully-practical, and Biblically-sound presentation of a Christian worldview that takes seriously the reality and nature of spiritual warfare and its irreplaceable role in the Christian life.

Through penetrating reflection questions, practical tips, and other interactive elements, this study guide invites individuals and groups to the real-life, intentional application of God's truth that promises to ground them in their Christian identity, embolden their exercise of Christ's authority, increase their discernment of God's voice, and propel them toward greater levels of victory and freedom in their ongoing struggle with the "world, flesh, and the devil". As a pastor, I anticipate the renewing impact this material will have as we share it with our congregation. For that matter, I believe any sincere believer who engages with this material will be better equipped, deeply inspired, and more fully empowered to overcome the challenges they face. Take the dive into this Study Guide and prepare to unlock and experience the victorious life to which Christ calls you.

Dr. Ken Bringas
Director, Life Pacific Seminary
Lead Pastor, New Life Foursquare Church

Dedication

I humbly dedicate this Study Guide to the many who have read my book, "Victorious Spiritual Warfare, So Simple, Grandma Can Do It," and asked for more.

I also dedicate this work to my beloved husband, Lance, and our cherished family. To Michael Stickler, Faith Burns, and their expert team at Leadership Books. To Kelly Tate, Brooke Turpin, and Maiah Mondy for their added wisdom and practical suggestions. To my pastors, many friends, and our church family at New Life Foursquare Church, who have lovingly prayed for and encouraged me to bring this Study Guide from dream to reality.

Thank you, Lord, that You've attended my writing, and for every one of these who came alongside me.

Maureen Broderson

CONTENTS

How To Get the Most Out of This Study Guide vii

Helpful Tips as You Begin ix

GOING DEEPER INTO:

CHAPTER 1: Introduction & The Unseen War
in the Spiritual Realm 1

CHAPTER 2: It Wasn't the Tuna Salad! 9

CHAPTER 3: You've Got Your Keys, Right? 15

CHAPTER 4: Eradicating Unbelief 23

CHAPTER 5: Hearing God's Voice 31

CHAPTER 6: The Believer's Authority and Power 39

CHAPTER 7: The Pursuit of Freedom 47

CHAPTER 8: Multiple Streams of Deliverance 55

CHAPTER 9: Be Not Ignorant 65

CHAPTER 10: Could I Possibly Be My Own
Worst Enemy? 75

CHAPTER 11: Discovering the Freedom
That Flows from Calvary 83

CHAPTER 12: The Warrior's Life of Freedom
& Conclusion 93

HOW TO GET THE MOST OUT OF THIS STUDY GUIDE

This interactive Study Guide has been created for individual or group study or in a weekend retreat setting. It is designed to work hand in hand with the book *"Victorious Spiritual Warfare, So Simple, Grandma Can Do It,"* and the chapter-by-chapter Filmed Teaching Series. Use the "Reflection" page at the end of each chapter of the Study Guide to make note of additional insights and thoughts the entire section has prompted. Consider your Study Guide and accompanying resources tools to look deeper into the truths found in God's Word concerning God's intention for you to live a life of victory; to know triumph over any negative habits in your life and over the darkness of our common adversary.

As you engage each chapter, pray that God will speak to you as you consider and respond to each question. Doing so will give you the opportunity to discover more about yourself along with the deeper dimensions of the fullness of God's intention and purpose for you to live out your life in the freedom Christ gave His life to provide for you.

Most assuredly, Jesus never intended for His creation to be people who cope with life. Instead, He created us to be people who conquer. He issues an invitation to us to share in the miraculous outcome of His victorious life, death, and resurrection in every area of our lives. Here's the first question, "Will you accept God's invitation?"

Let's go deeper together!
Maureen Broderson

HELPFUL TIPS AS YOU BEGIN

- **For Individual Study:** Begin each chapter in prayer, asking God to speak to you from His Word and the book.
- Before you engage the questions in this Study Guide, read the corresponding chapter in *"Victorious Spiritual Warfare, So Simple, Grandma Can Do It!"* Then, complete the Study Guide.
- Write your answers to the questions in the space provided or in a journal. Writing out your responses will give you clarity and a deeper understanding of yourself, God's Word, and the Lord's good plans and purposes for you.
- Then, watch the corresponding Filmed Teaching Episode. As you watch, use the "Reflections" page at the end of each chapter to make notes of additional insights and thoughts. Afterward, go back and ponder your responses to the Study Guide questions.
- Conclude each chapter as you began, with prayer. Give the Lord thanks for what He's teaching you and ask Him to lead you into specific ways to apply what you've learned.
- **For Group Study:** The Individual Study tips will also serve each participant in a group study. If you are facilitating a weekly group study or a spiritual warfare retreat, reviewing these tips with your participants will be of value.
- Before your first gathering, ensure each participant has their own Study Guide. Ask each person to come

prepared, having read the chapter in the book "*Victorious Spiritual Warfare, So Simple, Grandma Can Do It*," and answered the Study Guide questions for that chapter.
- I recommend that each participant agree to keep personal information shared by your members confidential. Doing so will create a safe place of trust for authentic discussion.
- Encourage each participant to gather with an open heart to engage the Video Teaching Episodes. Afterward, ask your participants to share the most impactful elements, their responses to the Study Guide questions, and additional personal reflections with one another.

GOING DEEPER INTO THE INTRODUCTION AND CHAPTER ONE:

The Unseen War in the Spiritual Realm

To get the most value out of these materials, read the Introduction and Chapter 1 of the book Victorious Spiritual Warfare, So Simple, Grandma Can Do It, complete this chapter of your Study Guide, and then watch the first Filmed Teaching Episode.

"...overwhelming victory is ours through Christ who loved us" (Romans 8:37b, *NLT*).

In the Foreword of *"Victorious Spiritual Warfare, So Simple, Grandma Can Do It,"* Dr. Robert Rohm comments, "When I became a Christian many years ago, I was basically taught that God loved me and had a wonderful plan for my life. It sounded like I was about to embark on an exciting, uplifting adventure. Eternal life was the gift of God through Jesus Christ our Lord (Romans 6:23). I was so happy! I think I had the feeling like that of getting on a cruise ship. Looking back, I now believe I would have been better served if I had been *warned that I was entering a whole new realm. The world, the flesh, and the devil are all real. I should have been told I was getting on a battleship!"*[1]

1. What thoughts, feelings, or observations from your own life come up for you as you consider Dr. Rohm's experience?

   _____

   _____

   _____

2. How does your life experience align with your initial expectations of being a follower of Christ?

   _____

   _____

   _____

The purpose of this first chapter of our Study Guide is to introduce spiritual warfare and advance your biblical understanding of the nature of the battle and the astonishing role God calls you to play in it. You'll explore the reality of the Lord's intention for His followers to challenge the enemy and victoriously overcome him. Remember this: God never intended for us to be people who cope. Instead, He created each of us to be people who conquer!

3. Throughout your life experience, what are some ways your adversary, the devil, has sought to stand in opposi-

---

[1] Maureen A. Broderson, *Victorious Spiritual Warfare, So Simple, Grandma can do it!* (Washington D.C, Vide Press, 2021), xiv.

tion to what you believe God's plan and purpose for your life truly is?

_____

_____

_____

Reading from the English Standard Version of Romans 8:37, the word "*conquerors*" is used. *"No, in all these things we are more than conquerors through Him who loved us."* In the original text of Scripture, "*conqueror*" means "to be completely and overwhelmingly victorious— to be completely victorious, to have complete victory over."[2]

4. What was your first thought as you read the definition of "conqueror"? Do you honestly believe God created you to walk out your life as a conqueror over the things of darkness?

   _____

   _____

   _____

   Why or why not?

   _____

   _____

   _____

---

[2] Johannes P. Louw and Eugene Albert Nida, *Greek-English Lexicon of the New Testament: Based on Semantic Domains* (New York: United Bible Societies, 1996), 500.

5. Read Ephesians 6:12. Where and with whom is God telling us the battles we face are really taking place?

_____

_____

_____

Sometimes, it's challenging to truly grasp a threat that comes against us from the realm of the unseen. As this Scripture confirms, a great war is being waged in the spiritual world, one greatly influenced by the forces of evil. We have a very real adversary who seeks to distort our true identity in Christ, bring chaos into our lives, plant doubt in our hearts, and disrupt God's plan and purpose.

6. How might Satan distract you to focus your "fight" not against him but elsewhere?

_____

_____

_____

Reading through the Gospels, we observe that one-third of Christ's earthly ministry involved confrontation between the Kingdom of God and the kingdom of darkness. As followers of Christ, this is an action that we cannot afford to ignore.

7. Read the following passages of Scripture and make brief yet specific observations about Jesus' attitude, His posture, His actions, His words, and the outcome as He faced down the enemy:

(a) Mark 1:21-27

_____

_____

(b) Mark 5:1-13

_____

_____

(c) Mark 9:14-29

_____

_____

(d) Luke 4:40-41

_____

_____

8. *As you consider your observations of Christ's posture, attitude, action, and outcome in opposition to the realm of darkness, how does that perhaps change your understanding and perspective of His words spoken to His followers in John 14:12 "Truly, truly, I say to you, whoever believes in Me will also do the works that I do; and greater works than these will he do, because I am going to the Father."?*

_____

_____

_____

9. Do you feel equipped for the battle? Do you perceive anything that might be holding you back?

   _____

   _____

   _____

10. Take a minute and think of a problem you may be currently experiencing, something that seems impossible to change or overcome. Then, looking through the lens of Christ's example and His words to you, how might you shift your perspective to see it as an exciting opportunity to partner with God and exercise the power He has given you to overcome the challenge?

    _____

    _____

    _____

As you conclude this first chapter, I encourage you to spend some moments in prayer, adding your own words to these ~ *Father God, I thank you that day by day, You are transforming me into the image of Your Son. Help me to remember to say the things that Jesus said, and by the power of Your Spirit, to do the things He did, all for Your glory, Amen.*

REFLECTIONS ON THIS CHAPTER *AND* FILMED TEACHING EPISODE 1

GOING DEEPER INTO CHAPTER TWO:

It Wasn't the Tuna Salad!

To get the most value out of these materials, read Chapter Two of the book Victorious Spiritual Warfare, So Simple, Grandma Can Do It, complete this chapter of your Study Guide, and then watch Episode 2 of the Filmed Teaching Series.

The Lord has *"called [us] out of darkness into His marvelous light"* *(1 Peter 2:9, ESV).*

1. After reading the true story of a pastor's dinner party gone terribly wrong, recall a time when you may have "jumped the gun," rushing to fix a problem because you thought you knew what was going on without first seeking God for His wisdom and strategy.

   _____

   _____

   _____

2. What was the outcome?

_____

_____

_____

Our lives are filled with moments or, at times, prolonged seasons when we experience peace and order. But then there are those times when things feel chaotic and entirely out of control. As you may have heard it said, "The good, the bad, and the ugly."

When faced with unexpected circumstances, things we didn't see coming, we often quickly jump to conclusions about the actual problem and what to do about it. We think we know what went wrong and the best resolution, only to discover later that our assessment of the problem and our remedy weren't the best at all. In those times, just like the situation we read about in Chapter Two of the book, the solutions we come up with on our own can result in pain, discomfort, expense, etc., for us and others. Regretfully, all too often, the people who end up being hurt the most are ourselves and those we love.

We see in God's Word that King David put his trust in God's guidance, assured that doing so would lead to blessing. He declares, *"You will show me the path of life; In Your presence is fullness of joy;' At Your right hand are pleasures forevermore"* (Psalm 16:11, NKJ).

Most scholars believe that David also wrote Psalm 119. Read Psalm 119:1-24.

Solomon, David's son, who later became king of Israel, also counsels us to *"Trust in the Lord with all your heart and lean not on your own understanding; In all your ways acknowl-*

edge Him, and He shall direct your paths" (Proverbs 3:5-6, NKJV). Scripture records in 1Kings 3:12 that God, responding to Solomon's prayer for an understanding heart (see 1Kings 3:7-9), declared of Solomon's wisdom and understanding, *"There has not been anyone like you before you, nor shall any like you arise after you."* In 1Kings 4:31, Solomon is called *"wiser than all men."*

3. *From these passages of Scripture, what do you observe that David and Solomon have in common?*

_____

_____

_____

4. *When it comes to making decisions about the challenges and dilemmas you face in life and who or what the cause of your problems might be, what value do you see in humbly inquiring of the Lord in prayer, asking for His wisdom, strategy, and solution before acting on your own?*

_____

_____

_____

As followers of Christ, we have stepped into life in the Kingdom of God. While it is an unseen reality, it is a very real supernatural reality, and we need the guidance the Lord assures us He will give us when we seek Him. We simply can't depend on our limited human understanding if we are to experience the abundant, victorious life Jesus promised us when He said, *"The thief does not come except to steal, and to kill, and to destroy. I have come that they may have life and that they may have it more abundantly"* (John 10:10, NKJV).

The simple truth is that things don't work out as we hope or plan for many reasons. The dilemmas and challenges in life originate from a number of sources. Our own mistakes, poor decisions we make, decisions others make for us, and the distractions of the world around us, to name a few.

We also face opposition from the enemy. And then there are times when God will hinder us from doing something He knows is not in our best interest. We put ourselves at risk when we guess at the cause of our dilemmas and move ahead without first seeking the Lord's understanding, wisdom, and timing before we act.

5. *Have you ever experienced a "closed door" that kept you from moving ahead with something and later realized it was God's hand of protection that closed the door? Describe the events and the outcome.*

_____

_____

_____

The Lord is calling you today to deeper dimensions of trust. Out of the vastness of His love for you, you are assured that He always has your good in His heart and mind. He is trustworthy, and the bottom line is that He's the only One who truly sees what's going on behind what you see with your natural eyes.

6. *What is your most significant "takeaway" from this chapter's study? And how will you put it into practice in your life?*

_____

_____

_____

As we conclude this chapter in our study, I pray for you the prayer the Apostle Paul prayed for the church in the city of Colosse. *"...asking that you may be filled with the knowledge of His will in all spiritual wisdom and understanding"* (Colossians 1:9b, ESV). *Lord, give us Your eyes to see and Your heart to know. Thank You for continuing to prepare and equip us to live fully into the destiny You created us to fulfill. In Jesus' name, Amen.*

REFLECTIONS ON CHAPTER TWO *AND* FILMED TEACHING EPISODE 2

GOING DEEPER INTO CHAPTER THREE:

You've Got Your Keys, Right?

To get the most value out of these materials, read Chapter 3 of the book Victorious Spiritual Warfare, So Simple, Grandma Can Do It, complete this chapter of your Study Guide, and then watch Episode 3 of the Filmed Teaching Series.

> *"And I will give you the keys of the kingdom of heaven, and whatever you bind on earth will be bound in heaven, and whatever you loose on earth will be loosed in heaven"*
> (Matthew 16:19, *NKJV*).

My husband and I each have our own keychains. If you look closely, you'll notice they have the same keys on them. Keys to our home, our cars, our mailbox, etc. Why? Because we are one, I'm his bride, and he's my bridegroom. So, we share the right of entry, authority, and access to the things God has entrusted to our care.

This is a picture of what is true of our relationship with the Lord as well. As His sons and daughters, we have the promise that Christ has provided us with the keys to His heavenly kingdom, along with the extraordinary privileges therein.

Read Matthew 16:13-19.

In this passage of Scripture, Jesus inquires of His apostles, "Who do men say that I, the Son of Man, am?" (v. 13b), and "But who do you say that I am?" (v. 15b). It was the first time Christ had asked this question of the apostles.

1. What was Peter's response to Jesus' question?

_____

_____

_____

The late Reverend Matthew Henry observed, "Peter's answer is short, but it is full, and true...Here is a confession of the Christian faith,...This is the conclusion of the whole matter."[3]

In response to Peter's worshipful confession, Jesus declared the apostle's understanding was revealed not by his human knowledge but by Divine inspiration. Then Christ went on to say that this confession would be the foundation upon which He would build His church and gave Peter the keys of the kingdom of heaven.

Now read John 1:12. In the original text, the word "right," as used in this verse, has to do with the authority or right to act - ability, privilege, and capacity of delegated authority.

2. How does this verse of Scripture relate to Peter's confession and Jesus then giving him the keys of the kingdom of heaven?

---

[3] Matthew Henry, *Matthew Henry's Commentary on the Whole Bible: Complete and Unabridged in One Volume* (Peabody: Hendrickson, 1994), 1695.

_____

_____

_____

We realize the key that gives us access to the kingdom of heaven is recognizing that Jesus is Lord, the One who came to redeem the world, and putting our trust in Him. The kingdom of heaven is open to us because Jesus is the key to entering, as He said in John 14:6, *"I am the way, the truth, and the life. No one comes to the Father except through Me"* (NKJV).

There's no biblical record of the conversations Jesus might have had with His other disciples following this event. Still, we know that the keys of the kingdom of heaven and accompanying privileges were also extended to each of His disciples (see Matthew 18:18-19).

And so, once again, consider what God's keys of His kingdom provide for us. Right, authority, and access ~ based on our confession of faith and our personal relationship with Jesus as Savior and Lord, we have been given the right and authority to access all of heaven's resources to empower and equip us to navigate our earthly circumstances. We can live in victory over the enemy as the God of all heaven and earth has intended for us. Astonishing, isn't it?

With access to God's kingdom, there comes access to kingdom resources that are available to you to address all of your earthly situations. Because of Jesus Christ, heaven stands ready to assist you in every aspect of your life.

3. *What is your response to being entrusted with the keys to the Kingdom of God?*

_____

_____

_____

The keys of God's Kingdom have given us the capacity to victoriously engage the spiritual realm by the power of His Holy Spirit. We will only be effective in their use as we inquire of the Spirit for God's direction and timing. Then, putting the keys into action, we unlock the windows of heaven. The Lord does not compel us to use them. Instead, He waits for us to respond obediently. When we do, we're given the privilege and His power to implement on Earth heaven's decisions concerning the affairs of mankind.

4. *Does understanding what you've been provided with when Christ gave you, as His follower, the keys of God's Kingdom help you to engage the battles you face in the spiritual realm more confidently and boldly? In what ways?*

_____

_____

_____

One last thing before we move on. The binding and loosing Jesus speaks of in Matthew 16:19 is not as I initially thought. Perhaps you may have thought this too. Jesus wasn't saying, "Here you go, here's My keys. Whatever you want to do, go for it, and I'll make it happen." Through study and experience, I came to understand that He was saying quite the opposite. We are given the right, access, and authority to enforce Christ's victory on Calvary, binding what He has bound and loosing what He intends to be loosed on Earth as it is in heaven.

Read Ephesians 3:10-12. In this passage, God informs us of His eternal plan to fulfill all He accomplished in Christ Jesus our Lord.

5. In whose hands has God placed the responsibility to advance His plan?

_____

_____

_____

6. Who are you to make God's plans known to?

_____

_____

_____

7. In what ways has God empowered and equipped you to fulfill His intention?

_____

_____

_____

You'll recall that in this chapter of my book, I share something my dad used to say, "There is no neutral ground. You're either riding on the steam roller, or you're part of the pavement."[4]

---

[4] Ibid, Broderson. p. 19.

8. As you consider my dad's observation, read 1Peter 5:8 and Revelation 12:9. Keeping in mind the description of the enemy in these two Scriptures, in what ways do you think my dad's observation applies to spiritual warfare?

_____

_____

_____

I've defined spiritual warfare in this way: *"Spiritual warfare engages worship and prayer—the effective outcome of which is the manifestation of the rule of God, the reign of His power, and the revelation of His kingdom. It is the prayerful and intentional confrontation with the demonic in the authority and power of the Holy Spirit."*[5] With this definition in mind, you realize that as you engage the realm of darkness, you are implementing Christ's rule, His reign, and His power to reveal His kingdom and advance His completed work on Calvary into your daily experience.

Now read Romans 6:5-14 and 8:10-11.

9. In what ways does this definition of spiritual warfare and the Scriptures in Romans align with the statement, "As the children of God, we are not fighting for victory; we are fighting from victory!"?

_____

_____

_____

---

[5] Ibid., Broderson, p. 16-17.

10. Reflect on what God is teaching you about spiritual warfare and make note of some of the most significant things you've learned in our study thus far. And how will you apply your learning in your life?

_____

_____

_____

Let's close in prayer ~ Lord, I ask that You continue to reveal the fullness of Your purpose, intention, and destiny for my life. Teach me how to implement all that You have entrusted to me as Your child, that nothing of darkness will succeed in hindering me or convincing me to surrender Your destiny for my life. In the matchless name of Jesus Christ, my Lord, Amen.

REFLECTIONS ON CHAPTER THREE *AND* FILMED TEACHING EPISODE 3

GOING DEEPER INTO CHAPTER FOUR:

Eradicating Unbelief

To get the most value out of these materials, read Chapter 4 of the book Victorious Spiritual Warfare, So Simple, Grandma Can Do It, complete this chapter of your Study Guide, and then watch Episode 4 of the Filmed Teaching Series.

"Now He [Jesus] could do no mighty work there…And He marveled because of their unbelief" (cf. Mark 6:1-6, NKJV).

Have you ever, like me, caught yourself confessing faith, but when facing a challenge, you began to speak or act in unbelief?

Or how about this: you make one mistake, experience one failure, and then take that on as an identity. You begin to talk to yourself, saying things like, "I can't do anything right. Everything I touch gets messed up." Or "I am a failure." "I'll never amount to anything."

I won't ask you to write out your response to this question, but ask yourself, has this ever been your experience?

In Proverbs 6:2, we read, "You are snared by the words of your mouth; You are taken by the words of your mouth."

Our self-worth is an identity issue, and it's time to believe and echo the words the Lord says about who we are when we enter into a personal relationship with Him instead of believing, repeating, and being held back by the lies of the enemy. It is then that we will begin to live our lives in Christ. *"For as in Adam all die, even so in Christ all shall be made alive"* (1 Corinthians 15:22, NKJV).

You'll recall Chapter Four of *Victorious Spiritual Warfare, So Simple, Grandma Can Do It* begins with a story of a man who took what he believed to be an unattractive, perhaps worthless blanket that had been in his family for years to be professionally appraised. To his astonishment, he discovered his blanket had immense value. With this revelation, he instantly felt very different about his old blanket! But think about it…nothing about the blanket changed. What changed everything was the man's understanding of the truth of the significance and value of his blanket.

1. *Read the story of Noah found in Genesis Chapter 6, verses 1-22.*

    Considering that Noah had never seen a flood before, do you think it was difficult for him to believe what God was telling him and then build an ark as God instructed him?

    What kind of social pressure and possible ridicule do you imagine Noah faced as he built the ark?

    _____

    _____

    _____

What was the result of Noah's belief and trust in God?

_____

_____

_____

2. In Hebrews 3:19, we learn that unbelief kept an entire generation of Israelites from entering the Promised Land. What kind of behaviors do you think resulted from their unbelief?

_____

_____

_____

3. Are there any areas in your life where you have given a place to unbelief and doubted God? Pause and ask the Holy Spirit to reveal any behaviors that might be holding you back from experiencing all that God promises. Then, ask God to help you transform your unbelief into complete trust and dependence on Him. Make a note of what God's shown you.

_____

_____

_____

4. Read John 11:1-44. What do you observe about Jesus' reaction when Mary and Martha came to Him weeping

over the death of their brother Lazarus? What do you think caused Jesus' response?

_____

_____

_____

Review verses 4, 14-15, and 38-40. Do you think these verses seem to indicate that Jesus knew Lazarus would live even before He and the disciples arrived in Bethany?

_____

_____

_____

In what way might the Lord's response to Mary and Martha change the way you view Christ's heart for us to believe in Him and His love for us?

_____

_____

_____

5. Many of our spiritual ancestors in the Bible were blessed for their belief. In addition to Noah, whose story of belief in the promises of God can you draw inspiration from in this season of your life?

_____

_____

_____

As you recall, we explored the biblical perspective of glory in Chapter Four of the book. Once again, read Psalm 8:3-5. As His children, we bear God's image. God endowed you and me with glory so deep that all creation pales in comparison. It is a glory unique to each of us, just as our fingerprints are unique to us. A glory our hearts long to rediscover.

6. *Read 2 Corinthians 3:18. While we know that sin separated us from living in God's glory, how does He restore His glory in us?*

   _____

   _____

   _____

   What does the idea of living in God's glory mean to you, and are you living that way today?

   _____

   _____

   _____

7. *Read John 7:37-38. Where do rivers of living water flow from?*

   _____

   _____

   _____

8. We know that empowerment and equipping for spiritual warfare begins with each of us and then reaches beyond. How do you think an unqualified belief and trust in your identity in Christ and God's living water moving through you affects your life and ministry?

_____

_____

_____

My friend, God is calling you to trust and believe. Make no mistake; our unbelief doesn't limit God. But it can limit what God intends to do in and through each of our lives. Here's what I've found, the first and most significant element of victorious spiritual warfare is a steadfast belief and trust in God and the truth of His Word. We are called to believe His character and nature are unchanging, His faithfulness is never-ending, and He has a plan for our lives.

I believe God wants to assure you how highly He values you and that your past does not define your present or your future. Who you are is who God says you are. Your identity is found in Him.

9. Read 2 Timothy 1:8-9. Is there anything that keeps you from believing God's called you and had a unique purpose in His heart and mind for you to fulfill before time began?

_____

_____

_____

10. At the end of Chapter Four of *Victorious Spiritual Warfare, So Simple, Grandma Can Do It*, what did the story of the significance of the missing piece of the puzzle speak to you about the unique role God created you to fulfill in His grand story?

_____

_____

_____

Before moving on, I encourage you to pause and pray once again, "Lord, You ask me to believe in who You are and who You've created me to be. Help me not be like the people in Your hometown of Nazareth, robbed of the miraculous move of God because of their unbelief (see Mark 6:3-6). Forgive me for my unbelief, Lord. From this moment forward, I choose to engage life with the confidence of being Your representative and ask You to help me accurately reflect Your glory. Let me fearlessly advance Your kingdom on Earth as it is in heaven and overcome the darkness in Your name as I live out all You've called me to be and to do. In the matchless name of Jesus Christ, Amen."

REFLECTIONS ON CHAPTER FOUR *AND* FILMED TEACHING EPISODE 4

GOING DEEPER INTO CHAPTER FIVE:

Hearing God's Voice

To get the most value out of these materials, read Chapter 5 of the book Victorious Spiritual Warfare, So Simple, Grandma Can Do It, complete this chapter of your Study Guide, and then watch Episode 5 of the Filmed Teaching Series.

This chapter of our book begins with a Scripture found in John 10:27, recording Jesus' word to His followers, *"My sheep hear My voice, and I know them, and they follow Me"* (ESV). The Lord wouldn't have spoken these words had He not intended to speak and for His people to hear and follow Him.

1. Share a time when you've sensed God's voice speaking to you.

   _____

   _____

   _____

What was your response?

_____
_____
_____

2. *One of the enemy's strategies is to try to prevent or distract us from hearing God. How have you experienced the enemy doing that in your life?*

_____
_____
_____

3. *Why is hearing God's voice important to you?*

_____
_____
_____

Why is hearing God's voice especially important in spiritual warfare?

_____
_____
_____

As we continue to consider the importance of listening to God's voice and following His instructions to victoriously engage in spiritual warfare, read the account of Philip's experience on the road from Jerusalem to Gaza found in Acts 8:26–40.

4. *Without understanding the angel's instructions, what was Philip's response?*

_____

_____

_____

What was the outcome of Philip's obedience?

_____

_____

_____

Like Philip, when you don't know how to pray or can't understand what's going on, what does God promise you in Romans 8:26-28?

_____

_____

_____

Over the years, I've learned that the keys to hearing God's voice are to come to Him with the expectancy that He will speak and that we will hear, our willingness to be changed by what we've heard, and our faith to believe that things will be changed around us by the power of applying God's Word.

Throughout the Gospels, Jesus repeated these eight words six times, *"He who has ears to hear, let him hear!"* (see Matthew 11:15; 13:9; 13:43; Mark 4:9; Luke 8:8; 14:35). And eight times in the book of Revelation Christ said, "*He who has an ear, let him hear what the Spirit says...*" (See Revelation 2:7; 2:11; 2:17; 2:29; 3:6; 3:13; 3:22; 13:9). Again, these would be meaningless exhortations if God does not expect to speak to us in ways we will be able to hear.

5. *When you come to the Lord in prayer, do you have a confident expectation that you will hear His response and a willing heart to respond?*

_____

_____

_____

If not, what stands in the way of your confident expectation and willingness to obey?

_____

_____

_____

While a healthy baby is born with the ability to speak and hear, we know there's much for a child to learn about talking and listening. It doesn't just happen the day they enter the world.

6. *What are some things you can learn and do to position yourself to hear God's voice?*

_____

_____

_____

As you've read in our book, God speaks to us primarily through the Bible, but at times, we also hear God's voice in our consciences, our circumstances, and through the wise and godly counsel of other people. By inquiring of God's Spirit and filtering what we see and hear through the Scripture, the Lord assures us we will hear His voice.

When listening for God's direction, we see throughout Scripture that we can't assume it will always be with an audible voice.

7. *What are some of the different ways you've sensed God's voice of assurance, confirmation, guidance, and direction?*

_____

_____

_____

I've also shared in my book that in addition to God's voice, there are other voices we hear daily ~ that of our own flesh in response to the world around us and the voice of our adversary.

8. *How do you distinguish between these voices, and how does God ask us to respond to each of them?*

_____

_____

_____

Another life lesson I've learned is that our loving God is far too wise to give us everything we ask for when we ask for it. There will be times when His response to your prayers is silence. But you never want to interpret His silence as His absence. Remember the words of Jesus, "...*I am with you always, even to the end of the age*" (Matthew 28:20b, NKJV).

9. In times of God's silence, is it difficult for you to continue to believe in His presence? What have you found to be most helpful to you as you navigate those times?

_____

_____

_____

The Lord asks you to trust Him, assured He will be with you while you wait. In His time, He will reward your faithfulness.

Let's once again close in prayer ~ *"Lord, thank You that You have created me in Your image and that I can know Your voice. May Your voice be the clearest of all the voices I hear. And as the Lord Jesus encouraged His followers, give me ears to hear and a heart to follow You. Fill me with the confidence of King David when he prayed, "You will show me the path of life; In Your presence is fullness of joy; At Your right hand are pleasures forevermore"* (Psalm 16:11, NKJV). *In the matchless name of Jesus Christ I pray. Amen.*

REFLECTIONS ON CHAPTER FIVE *AND* FILMED TEACHING EPISODE 5

GOING DEEPER INTO CHAPTER SIX:

The Believer's Authority and Power

To get the most value out of these materials, read Chapter 6 of the book Victorious Spiritual Warfare, So Simple, Grandma Can Do It, complete this chapter of your Study Guide, and then watch Episode 6 of the Filmed Teaching Series.

"And He called the twelve together and gave them power and authority over all demons and to cure diseases and He sent them out to proclaim the kingdom of God and to heal."
(Luke 9:1-2, *ESV*).

Begin by reading this passage in Luke 9 once again. After giving His disciples power and authority, but before sending them out, Jesus told them what they would have power and authority over. *"...all demons and to cure diseases..."*. It's essential to recognize that *"all demons"* refers to the spiritual realm, and *"to cure diseases"* refers to the physical realm in which we live.

1. *I invite you to pause and think about that. Isn't it astonishing to realize that as a follower of Christ, you have been entrusted with both God's power and His authority over both realms of your existence? What's your reaction to this incredible gift and responsibility God's given you?*

   _____

   _____

   _____

2. In my book, I observe, "Satan cannot steal your destiny. He can only try to make you give it up."[6] *After reviewing the realms over which God has entrusted His power and authority to you, what are your thoughts about this statement?*

   _____

   _____

   _____

To better understand all God's given us, let's begin by reviewing the definitions of "authority" and "power."

Authority is the right to rule; it's positional in nature. From a spiritual perspective, our position of authority is based on our personal relationship with Jesus Christ. By definition, "authority" carries the meaning of leave or permission; it's the right to give orders, make decisions, and enforce obedience.[7] Authority gives us the privilege, capacity, and freedom to rule

---

[6] Ibid., Broderson, 70.

[7] Ibid,, Broderson, 72.

on behalf of and under the directive of the one who's granted the authority to us.

3. In addition to the specific authority, we've examined related to spiritual warfare, what areas in your life have you been entrusted with authority?

_____

_____

_____

Power, on the other hand, is the ability to rule. It relates to might, strength, and force. Christ provides us with all the spiritual power of heaven and earth, the greatest and mightiest, standing out from the rest.[8]

It's critical to recognize it's God's power that goes before us and with us, not our own. And He commands us today, as He did Joshua, to be "*Strong and courageous! Do not be afraid or discouraged. For the Lord your God is with you wherever you go*" (Joshua 1:9b, NLT).

4. In what ways does God's command to Joshua, and now to you, increase your confidence and trust in God to address challenges in your life in God's authority and power?

_____

_____

_____

---

[8] Ibid., Broderson, 74.

As you've read in this chapter of our book, so that we may victoriously engage His authority and power, God hasn't sent us into battle empty-handed. The Lord's given us His armor to protect, defend, and stand against the enemy, and He equips us with His weapons to defeat the powers of darkness.

5. Read 2 Corinthians 10:4-5 and Ephesians 6:10-18. What is the Apostle Paul explaining to us about God's weapons and His armor?

_____

_____

_____

It's important to understand the effective utilization of God's armor and weapons are most assuredly dependent upon our responsibility to prayerfully inquire of the Holy Spirit for the revelation of His strategy and timing related to their use.

I invite you to consider this ~ unused weapons don't win wars in the physical realm, and armor stored in a closet somewhere will not provide you with the protection or equipment needed to fight a battle victoriously. The same is true in the spiritual realm. Passivity toward our enemy is what the devil wants from us.

6. Going forward, how will you implement what you've learned about God's armor and His spiritual weapons in the challenges you face in your life and the world around you?

_____

_____

One of the things I've learned about authority is that we cannot be in authority until we learn to live under authority. It is the Lord God almighty who has entrusted us with His authority and power, and our strength lies in our submission to His authority in our lives.

Let's not be confused. On our own, we don't have the authority or power to confront the demonic realm. As Dr. Jack Hayford taught, "Ours is the privilege, His is the power,"[9] The enemy will come at us with pride if we think differently.

7. *Read Acts 19:13-16. How will this understanding serve you as you ongoingly seek to guard against pride?*

_____

_____

_____

As we conclude this Chapter, I remind you that merely knowing about the authority God gives us, coupled with the vastness of His power He makes available to us, is exactly like what we've learned about the keys of His kingdom He's given us. Heaven's keys are of little benefit unless we choose to utilize them. The Lord asks us to believe His Word is true and to trust Him to fulfill it in and through us as we walk in His authority and power.

8. *Now, you have a choice to make. You can either lower the standard of Scripture to align with your life's experience thus far, or you can decide today to raise the standard of your life to align with God's Word. Which will it be for you?*

---

[9] Ibid., Broderson, 79.

_____

_____

_____

9. Is there a challenging circumstance in your life where this shift in perspective has the potential to make a positive difference in the outcome?

_____

_____

_____

One more thought before we pray ~ Two of my grandsons play Little League baseball. One is a pitcher, and the other a catcher. I may be slightly biased, but they're both great in their respective positions.

As I watched one of their games, observing the unique roles each played, I wondered ... is God calling His people to stop "playing catcher" on the ballfield of life, reacting to life's circumstances as they come? Could the Lord be saying that now is our time to step up and onto the pitcher's mound? To be the one with the ball in our hands, throw the strikes against our adversary, and advance the plans and purposes of the Kingdom of God in the world in which we live? I believe so. Do you agree?

It's much like the Lord's call to us not only to take possession of His Kingdom keys but also to pick them up and use them to unlock doors the enemy has attempted to keep closed. Then, to step through those open doors in His authority and with heaven's infinite power to advance the fullness of God's purposes on Earth as it is in heaven.

Let's bow our hearts together in prayer ~

Lord, thank You for the authority and power You've entrusted to me. Help me faithfully represent You with uncompromised integrity as I humbly surrender to Your authority in all I do and say.

Strengthen me to never turn from the enemy in fear as he seeks to assault me and shift my focus away from You. Empower me to walk in upright character and faith, then in privilege and power, that I may effectively enforce Your glorious victory at Calvary to destroy the works of the devil. Lead me by Your Holy Spirit, Lord, that I may, in true humility, serve Your intention and fulfill Your purposes all the days of my life. In the name of my Lord and Savior, Jesus Christ, Amen.

REFLECTIONS ON CHAPTER SIX *AND* FILMED TEACHING EPISODE 6

GOING DEEPER INTO CHAPTER SEVEN:

The Pursuit of Freedom

To get the most value out of these materials, read Chapter 7 of the book Victorious Spiritual Warfare, So Simple, Grandma Can Do It, complete this chapter of your Study Guide, and then watch Episode 7 of the Filmed Teaching Series.

> *"The reason the Son of God appeared was to destroy the works of the devil"*
> (1 John 3:8b, *ESV*).

What hope and confidence this Scripture gives us! Jesus came to destroy the works of the enemy in every area of our lives.

1. Since becoming a follower of Christ, have you ever sinned in a way that you thought you never would again?

   _____

   _____

   _____

Describe your thoughts about your sin and how it made you feel.

_____

_____

_____

If you're like me, as a follower of Christ, you may have experienced that we may be dead to sin, but sin's not dead to us! While old habits don't just fall away once a person enters into a personal relationship with Jesus Christ, by His Spirit, Jesus gives us the power and authority to not only say "no" to the enemy who seeks to lure us into sinful behaviors but to "know" how to stand in victory over him.

2. *One of the first things we need to know as we pursue God's freedom is to identify our opposition. Read 1 Peter 5:8-9. What's the enemy doing, and what is God instructing us to do about it?*

   _____

   _____

   _____

3. *Read James 4:7 and Ephesians 4:27. The exhortations found in these two Scriptures are written to the church, emphasizing that believers can give ground in their lives to the influences of darkness when we sin. What are God's instructions to His followers?*

   _____

   _____

   _____

In the original text, "opportunity," as used in Ephesians 4:27, refers to a territory or dwelling place. This brings us to the question presented at the beginning of Chapter 7 of our book, "Can a Christian have a demon?" It's a question that's caused division in the Church for many years.

Throughout the Gospels, the Greek word *daimonizomai* is used for people who "have demons" and is at times translated as demon-possessed. However, scholars agree that *daimonizomai* does not convey the English concept of possession, either ownership or eternal destiny. The word would be more accurately translated as "under the influence of." As I shared in my book, I once heard it said this way: demons do not possess or own a follower of Christ. God owns them. They are His creatures, and He is their judge. If they inhabit His people, they have only squatter's rights. Though simply stated, it communicates an absolute, unqualified truth.[10]

When a follower of Christ sins, suffers intense abuse or a traumatic event, our adversary seizes the "opportunity" to step in and take a "place or territory" within them. The darkness is then able to influence one's soul (their mind, will, and emotions). The adversary will begin to affect their thoughts and/or behaviors and will never willingly leave. But once again, the spirit of a disciple of Jesus Christ is inhabited by the Holy Spirit and Him alone.

4. *I've also heard it said, "There is no evidence in Scripture of a believer being influenced by a demon." Read Matthew 16:13-20. Would you say Peter's reply to Christ's question confirms his belief that Jesus was indeed The Christ, the Son of God?*

---

[10] Ibid., Broderson, 91.

5. Now, continue to read Matthew 16:21-23. In verse 23, while Jesus responds to Peter, who does He specifically rebuke?

6. Read John 13:1-2 and verses 21-27. Who was it that influenced Judas, also one of Christ's disciples, to betray Him?

The truth is, even the most devoted followers of Christ can be influenced and manipulated by the realms of darkness. We know we can't life coach, counsel, or medicate a demon when that occurs. We have to do what Jesus did, and what He instructs us to do ~ we have to cast them out.

7. Read Mark 16:16-18. In these verses, what are some of the miracles Jesus said He would do through those who believe in and follow Him?

_____

_____

_____

As we discussed in our previous lesson, Jesus has given His followers authority and power to do as He did when He walked the earth. This brings us back to the Scripture with which we began, *"The reason the Son of God appeared was to destroy the works of the devil"* (1John 3:8b, ESV).

8. Read 1John 4:4 and 5:4. *What assurances do we have that the victory we seek is already ours in Christ?*

_____

_____

_____

We read Christ's words in John 10:10, *"The thief does not come except to steal, and to kill, and to destroy. I have come that they may have life and that they may have it more abundantly"* (NKJV). Jesus came to give His life to pay the penalty for our sins in full so that we could enjoy an abundance of blessings flowing from our relationship with Him as we walk our life on earth and on into eternity. (see John 3:16 and Romans 5:8).

As we read in John 14:6 (NKJV), *"Jesus said to him, 'I am the way, the truth, and the life. No one comes to the Father except through Me.'"* Do you, perhaps, know things about God but don't really know God because you haven't yet entered into a personal relationship with Him?

Accepting God's invitation to receive Jesus as our Lord and Savior, to receive forgiveness for all of our sins, and to receive the promise of eternal life with Him He freely offers is the only path to a life of freedom—freedom from the enemy's influence and the guilt, shame, and condemnation that often accompany life's traumatic events and sinful behaviors. It is the only way to the peace that surpasses understanding and unspeakable joy.

While salvation cannot be earned, it can be refused. To do so will lead to an irrevocable eternal consequence. As I did in my book, I share Christ's invitation to you, to step out of darkness and into His marvelous light (see 1 Peter 2:9).

If you want to receive God's forgiveness, enter into a personal relationship with Him right now and make Him Lord of your life, or if you've walked away from God and would like to return to an intimate relationship with Him, I ask you to pray the following prayer with me. There's no better time than the present.

> *"Dear Lord Jesus, I believe in Your love for me.*
> *I thank You, Lord, for the gift of forgiveness of sin You offer me now.*
> *I know I have sinned against You, and I am sorry.*
> *I ask for Your forgiveness. I believe You shed Your blood on the cross to pay the penalty for my sins in full and that You rose from the dead.*
> *Jesus, because You are alive forever, I ask You to come into my heart and live with me. Today, I choose to trust and follow You as my Lord and my Savior, and I receive Your forgiveness.*
> *Guide my life and empower me to love as You love and to live a life pleasing to You.*
> *In Your matchless name I pray, Amen."*

If you have prayed this prayer for the first time or prayed it as a point of rededication, you now walk the glorious path of life accompanied by the Lord God Himself, who promises, *"I am with you always, even to the end of the age"* (Matthew 28:20b, NKJV).

9. *How does the assurance of God's forgiveness of your sins, the promise of His presence with you here on earth, and life eternal with Him feel?*

   _____

   _____

   _____

   You'll want to remember this day ~ I encourage you to make note of the date.

   _____

   _____

   _____

10. *Spend some time in prayer thanking the Lord for all He's done for you. Also, ask God to remind you of some of the most significant things you've been learning in our study thus far. Make a note of them and how you will apply them in your life.*

    _____

    _____

    _____

REFLECTIONS ON CHAPTER SEVEN *AND* FILMED TEACHING EPISODE 7

GOING DEEPER INTO CHAPTER EIGHT:

Multiple Streams of Deliverance

To get the most value out of these materials, read Chapter 8 of the book Victorious Spiritual Warfare, So Simple, Grandma Can Do It, complete this chapter of your Study Guide, and then watch Episode 8 of the Filmed Teaching Series.

"And you shall know the truth, and the truth shall make you free." (John 8:32, *NKJV*)

1. Have you ever thought there was only one way to do something, only to later discover another way to do it that turned out to be even easier and led to a better outcome? Briefly share your story.

   _____
   _____
   _____

In over 50 years of walking with God, a couple of things I've learned about Him are that, thankfully, He's God, and I'm not, and He's really big and really smart, too! And so we realize we don't want to be too quick to put God in a box.

As I wrote in my book, in decades of involvement in deliverance ministries, I've met people worldwide who believed the only way to experience freedom from the realm of darkness is to battle the demonic in confrontational prayer. In light of God's Word, that simply doesn't hold true. Let's look at some of the multiple ways the Lord delivers us ~ the streams of living water He provides for our freedom.

The first is "THE DELIVERING STREAM OF GROWTH IN TRUTH, THE WORD OF GOD."

2. Read John 1:1 and John 1:14. Who and what is the Word of God?

_____

_____

_____

3. Next, read John 8:31-32 and John 17:1-19. What does God's Word do for us, and how is knowing the truth found in His Word the foundation for our freedom in Christ?

_____

_____

_____

When you prayerfully and humbly engage God's Word, either by reading your Bible or sitting under the trustworthy teaching of His Word, God's life-giving, transformational power becomes available to you. When you open your heart to the power of His presence, you can and will experience that *"the word of God is living and powerful, and sharper than any two-edged sword..."* (Hebrews 4:12a, NKJV). His Word has the power to expose any influence the darkness has over you and set you free.

4. *Read Isaiah 55:10-11. What does God promise His word will do?*

_____

_____

_____

My friends, we are assured that "the Word of God contains within it the power to bring all it promises to pass."[11] It will transform you and set you free.

Next, look at "THE STREAM OF GOD'S LOVE."

5. *Read 1John 4:16. How does this verse describe the very nature of God?*

_____

_____

_____

6. *Continue in 1John 4 and read verse 18. What does this verse indicate God's love does?*

_____

_____

_____

---

[11] Ibid., Broderson, p.101.

In the original text, the word "perfect," as used in verse 18, means "complete," defining the completeness of God's love. The complete expression of God's perfect love in and through us as we extend it to others opposes and casts out every work of our adversary. It will not be fear alone that gets swept away.

To live in love and to love as God loves is to compassionately offer assistance, care, and concern to another. It is a love that's genuine and unconditional, without expectation of anything in return. By nature, this kind of love is the stream of God's living water that has the power to heal, deliver, and restore a person to wholeness.

7. How will you express the love of God to those around you?

    _____

    _____

    _____

Another pathway to God's freedom is found in "THE STREAM OF A SPIRIT-FILLED WALK IN WORSHIP."

8. Read Romans 8:1-6. These verses inform us that walking in step with the Spirit of God will bring freedom from condemnation and set believers at liberty from the dominion of sin. Is there any area in your life where the enemy is trying to bring judgment and condemnation upon you for a sin you've repented of and for which God has forgiven you?

_____

_____

As followers of Christ, the Lord will empower us by His Spirit to live a life not hindered by the effects of sin. But the residue of harmful habits most often remains in our lives because of the things we gave ourselves to before we knew the Lord or traumatic events in our lives.

9. *Read Galatians 5:16-21. Are there any works of the flesh described in these verses that continue to oppose your walk in the Spirit of God?*

_____

_____

_____

10. *Now read Galatians 5:22-26. To be filled with the Spirit of God and to walk in His power is as much a call to demonstrate His character as it is to align our actions with God's desires. To walk in the Spirit is to walk along and remain on the path He lays down before you. How have you experienced the power of God's Spirit within you to help you continue to grow in your ability to walk in freedom and power with Him?*

_____

_____

_____

As I wrote in *Victorious Spiritual Warfare, So Simple, Grandma Can Do It*, our Spirit-filled walk includes a life of worship. Worship is more than a song; it is our all-of-life response to the worth of who God is and all that He does. To worship is to center our mind's attention and our heart's affection on God.[12]

11. *Read Psalm 22:3-4. We see that God inhabits the praises of His people. These verses assure us that the entry of His presence is the enthronement of His power. Describe a time you sensed God's presence and power with you as you worshiped Him.*

_____

_____

_____

Your Spirit-filled walk of praise and worship will produce an atmosphere where God's divine presence resides. It becomes one of the most powerful defenses and devastating weapons in your earthy conflict with the enemy, as it welcomes God's majestic rule and reign into every circumstance of your life.

Lastly, let's look closer into THE DELIVERING STREAM OF AUTHORITATIVE PRAYER.

In the previous chapters, we've learned that we have been entrusted with God's authority and power to experience victory over the darkness. This victory comes as we follow the examples of Jesus' earthly ministry. We speak directly to the enemy and command, "In the name of Jesus, come out." Our authoritative prayers are the confrontation with the realm of darkness versus Truth and the power of God, spoken with authority.

---
[12] Ibid, Broderson, p.106-107

In Chapter One of this Study Guide, you read a number of Scriptures that revealed Jesus' confrontations with people who were influenced by spirits of darkness. Look back at your observations. Notice that never once did Jesus pray and say, "Father, I ask You to tell this evil spirit to leave." He spoke directly to the spirits of darkness, standing firmly in God's authority and power.

12. What are some of the words Jesus spoke to the unclean spirits He encountered that stand out most to you?

_____

_____

_____

13. Read Luke 11:20. As you engage in authoritative prayer, what are you bringing to bear on the realms of darkness?

_____

_____

_____

By our authoritative prayer, we enforce Christ's victory over Satan, implementing on earth heaven's decisions concerning the affairs of humanity. As we've said before, ours is the privilege, His is the power.

These are some of the ways God brings victory over the darkness. I'm confident I've not yet discovered them all. Truly, His thoughts and glorious ways are much higher than ours (See Isaiah 55:8-9).

As you conclude this chapter, spend some time in prayer, asking God, *"Grant to me, that with all boldness, I may speak*

Your word. Stretch out Your hands to fill mine to love and heal all those You bring before me. As I walk in worship and awe of You, may signs and wonders accompany all that You call me to do as You, the Deliverer, set Your people free. Through the matchless name of Jesus Christ, my Lord, I pray, Amen."

REFLECTIONS ON CHAPTER EIGHT *AND* FILMED TEACHING EPISODE 8

GOING DEEPER INTO CHAPTER NINE:

Be Not Ignorant

To get the most value out of these materials, read Chapter 9 of the book Victorious Spiritual Warfare, So Simple, Grandma Can Do It, complete this chapter of your Study Guide, and then watch Episode 9 of the Filmed Teaching Series.

> *"..that Satan will not outsmart us. For we are familiar with his evil schemes"*
> (2 Corinthians 2:11, *NLT*).

Military personnel and sports teams alike prepare for upcoming battles by studying their opposition's strengths, weaknesses, and patterns. With the goal of rising in confident assurance that the Lord of heaven's armies is with us in the spiritual battles we face and becoming the conquering champions God created us to be, in this chapter of our Study Guide, we will look at the tactics of our enemy. Doing so will enable us to build a solid offensive strategy and strengthen our defenses against the things of darkness.

1. *Share a time when you feared a situation, but when you learned more about it, you discovered there was no reason to be fearful.*

   _____

   _____

   _____

As I said in my book, ignorance of the enemy can only result in extreme vulnerability as you engage in spiritual warfare. In the words of Martin Luther, "On earth is not his equal." But as we've been learning, when we're on Calvary's ground, through the blood of Jesus Christ, our spiritual armor securely in place, and the weapons of spiritual warfare God makes available to us implemented, we need not be afraid.[13]

God's truth reveals we don't need to live in fear of the enemy. At the same time, through the Apostle Paul, the Lord reminds us in his letter to the church in Corinth that we're wise not to underestimate him either. *"So that Satan will not outsmart us. For we are familiar with his evil schemes"* (2 Corinthians 2:11, *NLT*). We need to acknowledge the power of darkness with the understanding and confidence of knowing that our adversary has no power greater than that of the Lord our God. So, let's deepen our understanding and learn more about who our common enemy is and some of his deceptive tactics.

2. *Animated by his unrelenting hatred of God, the New Testament identifies Satan by his purpose and activities. Read the following Scriptures, and write the description of the enemy found in each:*

---

[13] Ibid., Broderson, p. 109

(a) Matthew 12:24

(b) John 8:44

(c) John 12:31

(d) Ephesians 2:2

(e) Revelation 12:9-10

We could list many more Scriptures, but you get the point. There's a more comprehensive list in my book and several additional references in the filmed segment you'll engage for this chapter.

3. Why is it important to be aware of Satan's schemes?

This you can know for certain: the devil is mean; he hates God and all who are followers of Christ. He's persistent and never takes time off. Yet, you can also be confident that in the power of the Holy Spirit, and the anointing and authority God's placed on you, the devil won't succeed in his plans to be victorious over you.

4. *Read Ezekiel 28:14-17. What characteristics do you see that led to Lucifer's fall?*

___

___

___

We read in Psalm 89:14, *"Righteousness and justice are the foundation of Your [God's] throne; mercy and truth go before Your face."* The justice of God's character required Him to pass judgment on Satan.

5. *Read Revelation 12:9-10. What was the judgment of God on the enemy for his sin?*

___

___

___

6. *Read Revelation 12:13-17. In verse 17, who is our adversary, "the dragon," now at war with?*

___

___

___

There are multitudes of ways that Satan and his hosts of evil play out their tactics. Yet, upon closer examination, we see he most often repeats just a handful of strategies with minor variations to fit the circumstances. The devil has never had to change his tactics because, unfortunately, they're still effective.[14]

In Episode 9 of the Filmed Teaching you'll engage, I compare the temptation strategies of Satan in his encounter with Eve in the Garden (Genesis 3) and with Jesus in the wilderness (Matthew 4:1-11 & Luke 4:1-13). Therein, you'll observe the contrast between Eve's response to the enemy and the responses Christ modeled for us.

Encapsulated in these events, we see Satan's overarching schemes and strategies, those clearly identified by the Apostle John as 3 spiritual dynamics that he defines as the world's system.[15]

7. Read 1John 2:15-16. In verse 16, what are the 3 spiritual dynamics of the enemy that John defines as the world's system; those that operate in our world and encompass nearly all of the other strategies the devil employs?

_____

_____

_____

It's important to remember that temptation, in and of itself, isn't sin. The temptations we face tempted Jesus when He walked the earth as well. In Christ, we have a model of Godly responses to every temptation we encounter. We also have

---

[14] Ibid., Broderson, p.111
[15] Ibid., Broderson, p.113

the power of the Holy Spirit alive in us to empower us to resist the enemy's temptations and watch him flee, as is written in James 4:7, "Therefore, submit to God. Resist the devil, and he will flee from you."

All this to say, our decisions about our response to the temptations of darkness lead either away from sin or directly into it. Considering the temptations the enemy lays before us, we see they will nearly all fit into one of these 3 categories.

8. How does Satan use these 3 temptations to attempt to get a foothold in the lives of people?

_____

_____

_____

   (a) The lust of the eye ~ Are there things you've looked at that's gotten you in trouble?

_____

_____

_____

   (b) The lust of the flesh ~ Have some of the things you've desired – the things you thought would make you happy or ease your pain, resulted in more significant problems than you started with?

_____

_____

_____

(c) *The pride of life ~ Has insisting on your own way because you were sure you were right ever gotten you in a mess or damaged a relationship?*

_____

_____

_____

In all of this, we also see the multiple ways the enemy seeks to accomplish his primary goal – to get our eyes off Jesus. Everything the darkness throws at us is merely the means by which he seeks to achieve that goal and entice us to surrender our God-given authority to him, thus keeping us in bondage.

My friends, to be aware and alert to the enemy's tactics and then to stand firm against them in the power of the Holy Spirit is one of our most vital lines of defense in spiritual warfare. Walking in step with Christ, we can recognize and resist all these temptations of darkness as soon as they begin and not be tricked by our adversary's lies and distractions.

Also in Episode 9 of the Filmed Teaching accompanying this Chapter, I discuss several simple strategies Scripture sets forth for us to victoriously recognize and withstand the temptations of darkness. You'll want to make sure to watch it. Just briefly, here are a couple of them:

9. Read 2 Corinthians 10:5. What does God instruct us to do with the arguments that oppose the knowledge of Him?

_____

_____

_____

10. *Read Psalm 119:9-11. How did King David learn to keep from sin?*

_____

_____

_____

And one last funny but practical piece of advice I received from a wise and trusted pastor when I was being trained in spiritual warfare. I was told, "Maureen, sometimes you complicate and overthink things too much. Try this, just ask yourself, 'What would the enemy want me to do?' and then, do the opposite. He almost always overplays his hand, so if you then run your answer by the Holy Spirit for confirmation, you'll know what to do."

Remember, we're not in the middle of a game of tug-a-war on a horizontal playing field with the enemy. Satan is a created being, and this is a vertical chain of command with the Lord God almighty high above anything of darkness. And as God's word confirms, because of His *"great love for us,"* God has *"made us alive together with Christ...and raised us up together and made us sit together in the heavenly places in Christ Jesus"* (see Ephesians 2:4-6).

Let's conclude in prayer ~ *Lord, thank You for the truth of Your Word and that You have promised me Your presence, provision, purpose, and power. Thank You also for Your promise that "overwhelming victory is mine through Christ who loved us" (Romans 8:37b). Surround me with Your hedge of protection. I ask You to give me Your eyes to see and Your wisdom to recognize and stand against the evil plans of darkness against me, my family, and all that You've called me to be and to do. For Your glory Lord, Amen.*

REFLECTIONS ON CHAPTER NINE *AND* FILMED TEACHING EPISODE 9

GOING DEEPER INTO CHAPTER TEN:

Could I Possibly Be My Own Worst Enemy?

To get the most value out of these materials, read Chapter 10 of the book Victorious Spiritual Warfare, So Simple, Grandma Can Do It, complete this chapter of your Study Guide, and then watch Episode 10 of the Filmed Teaching Series.

"All of us used to live that way, following the passionate desires and inclinations of our sinful nature."
(Ephesians 2:3a, *NLT*)

Most of the time, I'm a kind person, so I won't present this as a question for you to answer. I don't know about you, but this Scripture is most assuredly true about me. There are times in my life that I've thought I could almost hear the enemy's laughter as he said, "Ha! I don't have to do anything to her; she's killing herself!" Oh, forgive me Lord. But, enough about me...

1. Read Psalm 139:23-24. What actions is David inviting the Lord to take with him?

_____

_____

_____

If you're a bit hesitant, let me share a couple of things I've learned about God over the years. First, when we come in humility before the Lord to confess our sins, we never tell Him anything about ourselves He doesn't already know. Secondly, God's presence is a safe place to let down our defenses, agree with God about what He already knows about us, and seek the freedom He freely and lovingly offers. These are moments when we are indeed running from death to life.

You may have seen as you've made your way through this study, there are times when our sinful thoughts, deeds, or actions give the darkness a point of entry into our lives.

In Chapter 10 of the book, you've read that there are also times when you become vulnerable to the enemy's oppression through no intentional action on your part. These occasions often result from traumatic events, accidents, severe emotional or physical wounding, illness, abuse, or even something as seemingly innocent as being overtired or when you're in pain.

2. In times of weakness and vulnerability, do you believe that if you inquire of the Holy Spirit, He will reveal any place the enemy has come in to take advantage of you? Why, or why not?

And we know no compassion or grace is found in the kingdom of darkness. The enemy will seize every opportunity to assail us. The significant point is that our response to these events in life is the decisive issue. While we cannot bear responsibility for the behaviors of others, we are most assuredly responsible for our own. Thankfully, we know that no matter our sins, God's love and forgiveness meet us right where we are when we come to Him in humbleness of heart and confess our ungodly behaviors.

3. *Do you also believe that by the authority and power God's entrusted to you, you can pray and command the enemy to leave any place he's begun to influence you? Once again, ask yourself, why or why not?*

Another thing to keep in mind is that when the enemy reminds us of our past failures and shortcomings, his intention is always to make us feel "less than," inadequate, unworthy, etc. But when God reminds us of these very same events in our lives, it's always for the purpose of extending His forgiveness, healing, and restoration. Some things may be challenging to look at in the moment, but the freedom God lovingly invites us into will always be worth it.

4. Look back at your answer to the 1st question in this chapter. As you engage the remainder of your Study Guide, are you willing to invite God to do these same things in you that he did in David? Will you welcome Him to expose any of the ways you've walked contrary to Him, either by your own choosing or your responses to things others have done to you?

_____

_____

_____

Our effectiveness in spiritual warfare begins with God's freedom realized in us, that the move of His Holy Spirit through us will not be quenched. Paul's letter to the infant church in Thessalonica instructs us, *"Do not quench the Spirit"* (1 Thessalonians 5:19, NKJV). According to Strong's (4570), in the original text, the word "quench" as used here means to extinguish, suppress, or thwart.

Let's consider some ways we might perhaps quench and basically pour water on the fire of the Holy Spirit, suppressing the power of His move in and through our lives.

We'll begin with unconfessed sin.

5. Romans 6:23 reveals that *"...the wages of sin is death..."*. What will be the result of unconfessed sin in your life?

_____

_____

_____

6. Now read 1 John 1:8-9. What has God lovingly given us as the remedy for the times we sin again?

_____

_____

_____

Now, let's look at unforgiveness. The issue of unforgiveness is an enterprise in that evil rises to hinder God's release of freedom in our lives and ministry to others as profoundly as anything else. We never want to forget God's gracious gift of forgiveness to us and allow unforgiveness toward others to restrict what God would do in and through us.[16]

7. It's been said that giving place to unforgiveness is like drinking poison and hoping the other guy dies. Read the Parable of the Unforgiving Servant in Matthew 18:21-35. What are the multiple ways Jesus teaches that the darkness of unforgiveness will take a toll on our bodies, minds, and emotions, quenching the move of God's Spirit in and through us?

_____

_____

_____

Moving forward, let's consider the way unbelief will obstruct God's miraculous power moving through us as we engage in spiritual warfare. You'll remember we dealt with unbelief in Chapter 4 of this study. But let's review one Scripture to re-

---

[16] Ibid., Broderson, p.126-127

mind us of the power unbelief has to quench the move of the Holy Spirit in and through us.

8. *Read Mark 6:5-6. We know that Jesus came to earth as a man, and Scripture verifies He didn't perform any miracles until the Holy Spirit came upon Him after His baptism (see Luke 3:21-22). In this passage in Mark, how did unbelief obstruct Jesus' ability to perform miracles?*

_____

_____

_____

In the previous chapter of your Study Guide, we discovered quite a bit about how pride will hinder the miraculous move of God. The Bible deals extensively with pride, for it is a severe hindrance to our spiritual life and freedom. Your vigilance against pride and commitment to maintaining a humble heart before God will most assuredly be one of the hinges upon which the door to successful and effective engagement in spiritual warfare will swing.

9. *What is your biggest "takeaway" from this chapter? Share why it is significant to you.*

_____

_____

_____

10. *How will this truth begin to shape the way you act?*

_____

_____

_____

There's so much more about the adverse effects of our thoughts and behaviors and God's redemptive plan for us in our book and the filmed teaching segment you'll engage. If you haven't yet read Chapter 10 of *Victorious Spiritual Warfare, So Simple Grandma Can Do It,* I highly recommend you do so, and be sure to engage the filmed segment for this chapter as well.

As you conclude this portion of your Study Guide, I encourage you to pause in stillness before the Lord and ask Him to speak to you and bring to your understanding any place where God's magnificent power and glory in you may have been quenched by your thoughts, behaviors, or negative experiences and your responses to each of these things. Please remember, the Lord only wants to remind you of these areas in your life because of the vastness of His love for you. He always does so with the intention to love, heal, and restore you. Embrace and respond to His revelation and thank Him for it.

Let's conclude together in prayer ~ *Lord, thank You for Your steadfast love for me. Thank You for loving me too much to let me stay the way I am, but instead continue to patiently and tenderly transform me more and more into Your image. Thank You for giving me Your eyes to see and Your ears to hear Your wisdom, revelation, and perspective. I welcome Your revelation that nothing of darkness will hide in the shadows of my soul to quench Your Holy Spirit and hinder Your freedom and purposes in my life. In Jesus' name I pray, Amen.*

REFLECTIONS ON CHAPTER TEN *AND* FILMED TEACHING EPISODE 10

GOING DEEPER INTO CHAPTER ELEVEN:

Discovering the Freedom That Flows from Calvary

To get the most value out of these materials, read Chapter 11 of the book Victorious Spiritual Warfare, So Simple, Grandma Can Do It, complete this chapter of your Study Guide, and then watch Episode 11 of the Filmed Teaching Series.

"You were dead because of your sins and because your sinful nature was not yet cut away. Then God made you alive with Christ, for He forgave all our sins. He canceled the record of the charges against us and took it away by nailing it to the cross. In this way, He disarmed the spiritual rulers and authorities. He shamed them publicly by His victory over them on the cross" (Colossians 2:13-15, NLT).

1. As you ponder this Scripture and all Jesus has done for you as His follower, what thoughts and feelings come up for you?

_____

_____

_____

Christ's sacrificial death on the cross, His shed blood, and resurrection triumph are the only grounds for our forgiveness, redemption, spiritual freedom, and restoration, as well as for the delegation of the Lord's authority and power to us as believers in Him. This is the foundation upon which all Kingdom privilege and power may be restored to humankind.

As we've continued to learn throughout this study, many of our sinful habits did not fall away when we came to Christ and surrendered to Him as Lord. After becoming a follower of Christ, we've all sinned again. And so, even as believers, there are places we've given ground to the enemy in our lives to influence our thoughts and behaviors (see Ephesians 4:22-27). We've also learned that God provides us with clear pathways to experience freedom from the enemy's grip in those places.

While there are no "checklist prayers" related to the "Stream of Authoritative Prayer" discussed in Chapter 8, Scripture reveals biblical principles for our prayer for ongoing freedom in Christ. We are called to repent, renounce, and break the enemy's hold. Lastly, so that the places vacated by the darkness are not left empty, tempting the enemy's return, we pray to fill them with God's glory.

And so our first step is that of repentance for our sins.

2. *Read the words of Jesus recorded in Matthew 9:13 and Luke 5:32. What did Jesus say He came to do?*

_____

_____

_____

True repentance may begin with being sorry for something you've done, but it also includes a decision to turn from sin and live to honor God. It's a change in the way we think about sin. Repentance begins in one's heart and is followed by our active response to act differently "...*and do works befitting repentance*" (Acts 26:20b, NKJV).

3. What would "works befitting repentance" in your life look like?

_____

_____

_____

Our next step to God's freedom is to renounce. To renounce means to give up a claim, to cut off, and to refuse further association. It goes a step further than repentance in that you actively take a stand against and reject both the sin and the spirits of darkness that have been given an opportunity in your life.

4. Read 2 Corinthians 4:2. In my book, I observe that when you repent, you're talking to God, and your posture is prayer. When you renounce, you're speaking directly to your enemies in the realm of darkness. You are rejecting the enemy's lies, and your posture is war.[17] Given what you've learned in this study, do you feel confident to take this stand against your adversary? Why or why not?

_____

_____

_____

---

[17] Ibid., Broderson, p. 136

The next step Scripture sets forth for our authoritative prayers is to break the chains that have held you in bondage and cast the darkness out of the places they were given to occupy. As a follower of Jesus Christ, you're empowered and equipped to do so in the authority Christ has given you and in the power of His name.

When you began this study, you looked at several passages of Scripture revealing how Jesus addressed the demonic realm when He walked the Earth. As a reminder, you may want to look back at Chapter 1 and review your responses to those Scriptures. We know after Christ's resurrection and ascension into heaven, he left His followers with a very full mandate for their lives.

5. Read Mark 16:16-17. What are the "signs" Jesus said would follow those who believe?

_____

_____

_____

We know, as believers, the authority and power Jesus demonstrated to destroy the grip of darkness in the lives of people He encountered, He has now entrusted to each of us. This truth is confirmed in His declaration recorded in Luke 10:19a, *"Behold, I give you the authority to trample on serpents and scorpions, and over all the power of the enemy ..."* (NKJV).

In my book, I addressed the destructive power of anger in our lives as a topic to demonstrate this Biblical pattern of authoritative prayer for freedom. In the filmed series you'll engage in for this chapter, I address another prevalent spirit of darkness in our world today: fear.

As you implement the principles in this Study Guide, it's essential to understand they apply to any area where the enemy has taken advantage of you and now imposes his influence on your thoughts and behaviors. What's critical for you at this point is that you inquire of the Holy Spirit as you come to a time of prayer for God's freedom in your life. Ask Him to reveal an area of your life in which God intends to set you free.

6. Read 1 Corinthians 2:9-12. What does God promise that He will do for you by His Spirit?

_____

_____

_____

My friends, the Lord your God loves you and wants you to be free from the influences of darkness. Christ longs for you to live in the abundant life He gave His very life to give you. In 1 John 3:8b, we read, "...For this purpose, *the Son of God was manifested, that He might destroy the works of the devil*" (NKJV).

Casting out the influences of darkness doesn't need to be something intimidating or frightening. Remember, you're empowered to do so in the power and authority you have in Christ. And the devil's not deaf, so you don't need to raise your voice. But he can't read your mind either, so you do need to speak.

For more detailed information about the principles of authoritative prayer, if you've not yet done so, you'll want to read Chapter 11 of *Victorious Spiritual Warfare, So Simple Grandma Can Do It*.

7. *Take the time to pray. Inquire of the Holy Spirit, asking Him to reveal an area in your life where you're being influenced or manipulated by the realms of darkness.*

   - *Then, follow the leading of the Holy Spirit and incorporate the principles you've just studied. Begin with humble repentance. Repent of listening to, agreeing with, or believing the devil's lies rather than God's promises of life, hope, and faith. Ask the Lord to forgive you for any specific sinful behaviors you've engaged in and any words you've spoken in agreement with the enemy's lies that have given place to the realms of darkness. Assured that God's word is true and He is faithful and just to forgive you for that which you've humbly and sincerely repented of, open your arms as a gesture of receiving His forgiveness and cleansing. Breathe deeply and cherish this moment.*
   - *Next, renounce any spirits of darkness that have influenced and manipulated your thoughts and behaviors. Speak directly to the enemies and declare your choice today to refuse further association with them. Then, pause and take a moment to take a deep breath.*
   - *And now, in the name of Jesus and in the authority He has given you as His child, declare that you break all ties with the spirit you're addressing. Take authority over the darkness and command it to leave you. Command the enemy to sever his destructive hold over you and declare everything raised against you from the realms of darkness, everything contrary to God's purpose in you, has been taken out of your way. In the Name above every name, that of Jesus Christ your Lord, every bit of darkness must go now. Amen.*

The Greek word for spirit is *pneuma,* which means breath. You most likely didn't feel these spirits of darkness enter you, and you probably didn't feel them leave either. Stop and take another deep breath, expelling any remnant of darkness and taking in God's glorious breath of life and freedom.

8. *Before taking your final step, read Luke 11:24-26. What does this passage inform you about the enemy's intention after he's been cast out?*

   _____

   _____

   _____

9. *Inquire of the Holy Spirit and ask Him to show you what God intends to fill the places vacated by darkness with so that they won't be left empty. Most often, it's the opposite of what you've just experienced freedom in.*
   For instance, if you had struggled with anxiety, God may whisper that He's filling you with His peace and trust. Now give voice to those things in prayer, receiving all God intends for you as you step out of darkness and into His marvelous light in the area you've prayed for freedom.

   _____

   _____

   _____

The enemy may whisper to you that this was all too easy or that you can't be rid of him with a simple prayer like this. Everything you've prayed you've also seen set forth in God's Word. Remember, the enemy is a liar.

Sometimes, after praying for God's freedom, people don't feel differently at all. But then, as the days go by, they begin to notice they're responding differently to situations in their lives. It's important not to judge the miraculous move of God in your life and the freedom He promises by your feelings in the moment.

10. *Read John 8:36. What does God promise you in this verse? How will you confidently rest in this promise?*

___

___

___

11. *God's Word in Revelation 12:11 tells us that "they overcame him (the enemy) by the blood of the Lamb and by the word of their testimony..." Will you share your glorious testimony of the freedom God's given you with someone to give them hope that God will overcome the darkness in their own life as well? Who comes to your mind?*

___

___

___

Let's close in prayer. *Father God, I thank You for Your glorious freedom. I ask You now, that by Your Spirit, You will strengthen me to apply the truths of Your Word and empower me to live in obedience to it, that I may resist the enemy and not be entangled again with the yoke of bondage in this area that You've miraculously and lovingly set me free from. Remind me to stay current with You, Lord, to quickly repent and turn away from sin. I love You Lord, and I thank You for the vastness of Your love for me. I give You all the glory God, for the freedom You've given me. May I live to honor You all the days of my life. Amen.*

REFLECTIONS ON CHAPTER ELEVEN *AND* FILMED TEACHING EPISODE 11

GOING DEEPER INTO CHAPTER TWELVE and the CONCLUSION:

The Warrior's Life of Freedom and In The Master's Hands

To get the most value out of these materials, read Chapter 12 and the Conclusion of the book Victorious Spiritual Warfare, So Simple, Grandma Can Do It, complete this chapter of your Study Guide, and then watch Episode 12 of the Filmed Teaching Series.

> "Stand fast therefore in the liberty by which Christ has made us free, and do not be entangled again with a yoke of bondage" (Galatians 5:1, *NKJV*).

At this point in our study, you've probably experienced that in a moment, God miraculously sets us free from the enemy's grip. As you read in our book, it's a freedom that can be pictured as an unlocked prison cell, the chains of bondage broken and the prison door thrust open.[18]

---
[18] Ibid., Broderson, p. 154.

Moving forward, it's important to remember that God's deliverance from the darkness never does away with our need for obedience to Him. Standing up, walking out of the prison of darkness, living in the freedom the Lord has given you and becoming the spiritual warrior He intends for you to be are life patterns of daily choices.

1. *Read Galatians 5:1. In this verse, what are the things the Lord is instructing you to do to maintain the freedom He's given you?*

   _____

   _____

   _____

As we all may have experienced, our bad habits and the power of untamed desires remain. God knew that. Thus, He has lovingly given us himself, His Holy Spirit to live in us, accompanied by the promise He will empower us to live a life of freedom.

2. *Read James 1:12-16. In life, what does God reveal as the primary source of our entanglement with sin? In what ways has this been your experience?*

   _____

   _____

   _____

The freedom God's given you has brought you back to a place of choice. In the future, each of us must choose daily to give careful attention to the principles found in God's Word.

There's a need for balance here. While God opposes legalism and the thought that our righteousness in Christ depends upon our efforts and can be achieved by fulfilling a list of do's and don'ts, the Lord asks us to guard against sin and to respect the liberty, freedom, and grace He extends to us.

Let's look at some of the ways we find in Scripture that will enable us to maintain our freedom in Christ and rise in the Spirit of God to become His champions in the spiritual battles we face.

- First, we inquire of the Holy Spirit.

3. *Read John 16:13-15. In what ways do you see Christ's promise of the Holy Spirit as the foundation of your ability to walk in freedom and to equip and empower you to be victorious in spiritual warfare?*

_____

_____

_____

- Another vital principle is to become a person of God's Word. Do you remember how Jesus responded to the devil's temptations when He victoriously stood against him in the wilderness? (See Matthew 4:1-11).

4. *Now read Joshua 1:8 and John 8:32. As you approach not only the Word of God in Scripture but the Giver of the Word himself, what are the promises God gives you if you commit to be a person of the Word?*

_____

_____

_____

How will you apply God's Word to the challenging circumstances you face?

_____

_____

_____

- Another pathway to victory in Christ is to become a person of praise, worship, and thankfulness. These characteristics are each mighty weapons God gives us in the spiritual battles we face, as they shift our focus from what we can't do, to remind us of what God can do.

5. *Read Psalm 22:3, wherein we see that the entry of God's presence and the enthronement of His power is found in our praise and worship. Where the presence of God is, there will be no place for the enemy. How will you grow deeper in becoming a person of praise, worship, and thankfulness?*

_____

_____

_____

- Another way God enables us to victoriously walk in freedom is to live in the fellowship of believers. As the people of God, we are the Body of Christ. One body, of which He is the head. Jesus loves His church, so much so that He gave His life for it ~ a body of believers that He refers to as His bride (see Revelation 21:9).

6. *Read Acts 2:42 and Ephesians 4:7-16. What are the characteristics of the early church as they gathered together, and what has God given to His church to empower and equip them "for the work of ministry?"*

_____

_____

_____

In light of these Scriptures, I encourage you to ponder this statement; "You cannot forsake the bride without forsaking The Bridegroom."[19] Oh, how we need one another! As King Solomon confirmed, "*As iron sharpens iron, so a man sharpens the countenance of his friend*" (Proverbs 27:17, NKJV).

- Another way God instructs us to walk in freedom is to walk in the Spirit.

7. *Read Galatians 5:16-26. What is God's promise to us if we will walk in the fullness of His Spirit? And what evidence will we see in our lives when we do?*

_____

_____

_____

We have seen in these principles that if we rely on our own talents, strengths, and abilities, we'll become vulnerable to the aggressive attacks of the adversary. God's intention has always been to empower and equip His people with His Spirit, which is precisely why Jesus commanded His disciples to "*wait*

---
[19] Ibid., Broderson, p.169-170

for the Promise of the Father..." to be *"endued with power from on high"* before they set out to fulfill His commission. (See Luke 24:49 and Acts 1:4,5 & 8).

8. Read Ephesians 3:16. How does God say He will strengthen us?

　_____

　_____

　_____

- Another biblical principle enabling us to walk in God's freedom is to live a life of forgiveness. You'll remember an extensive discussion about the damaging effects of unforgiveness in Chapter 9 of *Victorious Spiritual Warfare, So Simple Grandma Can Do It,* pages 126 - 130. You may want to go back and review that portion.

The bottom line is God calls us to a lifestyle of forgiveness and release, refusing anger, bitterness, and resentment. Ephesians 4:26-27 tells us, *"Be angry but do not sin. Do not let the sun go down on your anger. Do not give place to the devil"* (MEV). Also, decline from holding grudges and swiftly release offenses to the Lord.

9. Is there anyone currently in your life that God is asking you to forgive? If so, how will you respond?

　_____

　_____

　_____

In addition to these principles, in our book and Episode 12 of the Filmed Teaching Series you'll watch, you'll learn more about some additional ways God empowers you to live in His freedom. Each will empower and equip you to stand against the assaults of the enemy and to share the hope of victory over the darkness with those around you.

Moving forward, as I mention in the Filmed Teaching for this chapter, it's not my intention within this context to engage in the debate regarding the baptism with the Holy Spirit or speaking in tongues, topics that have caused tension and division within the Church for many years.[20]

However, I will assert that if the supernatural ministry of Jesus Christ is to be replicated in and through your life, He assures you, as He did His disciples, that His intention is for you to receive the power and enablement of the Holy Spirit (see Acts 1:5 & 8). As it concerns spiritual warfare, it is my belief and experience that to engage the unseen battle with the forces of darkness without the empowerment of the Holy Spirit and the fullness of His gifting would be comparable to stepping into a fierce military battle unarmed.

To quote Dr. Francis McNutt, "The answer is simply to look at the example of Jesus, who walked with God for thirty years, then needed a new dimension of union with the Spirit to empower Him for ministry. I need that subsequent empowering too."[21]

Thus, I invite you, just for a moment, to set aside any preconceived notions or positions you may have about the Holy Spirit.

---

[20] Ibid., Broderson, p.160-163

[21] McNutt, Francis, *Deliverance from Evil Spirits: A Practical Manual* (Grand Rapids: Chosen, 2009), 279.

10. Ask yourself the same question Paul asked, "some disciples" in Ephesus, "Did you receive the Holy Spirit when you believed?" So they said to him, 'We have not so much as heard whether there is a Holy Spirit.'" Paul went on to confirm their repentance, belief in Christ Jesus, and baptism in water, then "laid hands on them, [and] the Holy Spirit came upon them, and they spoke with tongues and prophesied" (see Acts 19:1-6). Are you hesitant to ask the Lord to fulfill this promise in you? If so, why?

_____

_____

_____

It seems Jesus knew that for His followers to move beyond their natural humanity and victoriously engage in spiritual warfare, they would need the vibrant power of the Holy Spirit in the most extraordinary measure.

God leaves the decision with you. If you have not been baptized with the Holy Spirit since you have believed and sense it is something the Lord is calling you into today, I encourage you to bow your heart with me and pray this simple prayer:

Dear Lord Jesus, I thank You and praise You for the vastness of Your love and faithfulness to me. My heart is filled with joy as I ponder the great gift of salvation You have freely given me.

I come in humility and glorify You, Lord Jesus. I now also come in obedience to Your call. I desire the fullness of the Holy Spirit. Because You have washed me from my sins, I thank You for making the vessel of my life a worthy one to be filled with the Holy Spirit of God.

I want to overflow with Your life, love, and power, Lord Jesus. I long to show forth Your grace, Your Words, Your goodness, and Your gifts with those I encounter daily. So, in simple childlike faith, I ask You, Lord, to fill me with the Holy Spirit.

I love You, Lord, and I lift my voice in praise to You. I trust You, Jesus, and welcome Your Spirit to manifest Your might, dominion, and miracles in and through me for Your glory. Thank You, Lord, and Amen.

If you have partnered with me in this prayer, you have invited Jesus to baptize and fill you with His Holy Spirit ~ AND HE HAS![22] Praise Him and allow the Holy Spirit to come and enrich your understanding of what He has done for you in these moments. Magnify Him, love Him, trust Him, and leave the rest to the Holy Spirit.

As we've been learning, in the final analysis, our spiritual life is one of simple moment-to-moment dependence upon Jesus and the revelation and guidance of the Holy Spirit. The Holy Spirit will empower us to walk in step with Him.

As we come to the end of our study, I want to briefly share the true story from the conclusion of our book, that of the creation of Michelangelo's magnificent statue of David. You'll also learn more about the events that transpired in its creation in the filmed teaching segment accompanying this chapter.

To briefly summarize, two acclaimed artists had failed in their attempts, determining the piece of marble they had to be fractured, damaged, weakened, and in their eyes, useless. It was subsequently stored in a dark room in the back of a chapel for over three decades. Being approached by the City Fathers of Florence, Italy, the young Michelangelo agreed to complete the project. For three years, this master craftsman labored tirelessly.

---

[22] Jack W. Hayford, *Penetrating the Darkness* (Bloomington, MN: Chosen, 2011), 187-188.

And we know the result. For centuries, thousands have been blessed by Michelangelo's astonishing portrayal of David. At the hands of a master ~ that which was thought to be useless became priceless, worthless became treasured, cast aside became valued beyond measure, mistakes redeemed, and fractured became whole.

11. *Have there been times in your life when you felt useless, worthless, cast aside, full of mistakes, or fractured?*

_____

_____

_____

No matter what your past has held, you are assured the Lord your God, who has *"fearfully and wonderfully"* formed you with His own hands (see Psalm 139:14-16), promises in this same way to redeem you, restore you, guide you, empower and equip you to be the person He created you to be. That when you trust your heart and life into His loving hands, you will become a reflection of His light, His life, and His love.

Even more than you want it for yourself, God's desire is for you to fulfill all He has had in His heart and mind for you since before time began. That you will conquer the things of darkness you face in life and be His representative to bring the glory of heaven to earth in every circumstance you encounter, for His glory.

12. One last question: are you encouraged to know that in God's eyes, your past does not determine your present or your future?

_____

_____

_____

As you conclude your study, join me in prayer once again ~ I surrender to You, Lord, and thank You for all You've taught me and will continue to teach me as I seek You. Thank You for commissioning and equipping me to defeat the evil one as I impose Your victory on Calvary in every situation in my life.

Thank You for redeeming me from an empty way of living. I pray that You will continue to heal and restore the fractures in my heart, mind, and emotions caused by the shrapnel of a world gone terribly wrong. Then, bring me to a place of more confident trust in You.

Thank You for restoring my hope, Lord ~ hope for the future and my ongoing freedom. Hope for the generations that will follow me and for the world in which I live. I entrust my life to You, the One who made me. May I go forward to victoriously accomplish the most extraordinary privilege that life will ever hold, that of stepping into the unique role that You created me exclusively to fill. May my life never be the same, but each day, lovingly shaped by Your hands, more into Your image. In the matchless name of Jesus Christ, my Lord, I pray. Amen.

As I did in my book, I leave you with one final word of encouragement. Ask the Holy Spirit to give you His eyes to see that which your natural eye cannot see. Oh, not just the darkness, but more importantly, to see yourself as He sees you, and His magnificent, penetrating light, that you may behold and share His glory.

In the days ahead, I pray that you will continue to discover the warrior's strength and effectiveness against the darkness of the times in which we live. You were born for such a time as this! May it also be the place where you will experience His perfect peace, contentment, and the joy of the Lord your God. May God's most lavish blessings attend all you set your hand to. In His glorious name I pray, Amen.

REFLECTIONS ON CHAPTER TWELVE, *the* CONCLUSION, *AND* FILMED TEACHING EPISODE 12

TO CONNECT WITH
MAUREEN BRODERSON

Search Online for
"Author Maureen Broderson"

Speaking Events
Books
Contact
Other Resources

or you may scan below
QR Code